Faces of NASCAR

A Pictorial Tribute to America's Greatest Sport

Scott Robinson

First published in 2006 by MBI Publishing Company and Motorbooks, an imprint of MBI Publishing Company, 400 1st Avenue North, Suite 300, Minneapolis, MN 55401 USA

Motorbooks titles are also available at discounts in bulk quantity for industrial or sales-promotional use. For details write to Special Sales Manager at MBI Publishing Company, 400 1st Avenue North, Suite 300, Minneapolis, MN 55401 USA.

To find out more about our books, join us online at www.motorbooks.com.

ISBN-13: 978-0-7603-2440-0

Editor: Leah Noel
Designer: Mandy Iverson

Printed in China

Library of Congress Cataloging-in-Publication Data

Robinson, Scott.
   Faces of NASCAR / Scott Robinson.
     p. cm.
   ISBN-13: 978-0-7603-2440-0
   1. Stock car racing--United States--Pictorial works. 2. NASCAR (Association)--
Pictorial works. I. Title.
GV1029.9.S74R63 2006
796.720976--dc22

                2006007836

On the cover: From left, (top row) 2005 NASCAR NEXTEL Cup champion Tony Stewart;
fan Jim Long of Ellicott City, Maryland; driver Kasey Kahne; (bottom row) Jeff Gordon
fan Ben Sanders of Wichita, Kansas; team owner Jack Roush; tire specialist Lisa Smokstad.

On the frontis: Richard Petty's signature belt buckle, which celebrates his record seven
NASCAR NEXTEL Cup championships.

On the title page: A fan wearing his favorite NASCAR hat keeps an eye on the garage area,
waiting to catch a glimpse of his favorite driver and team.

On the back cover: Drivers and longtime friends Dale Earnhardt Jr. and Matt Kenseth share a lighter moment in the garage.

Contents

Introduction
Racing Isn't Just About Speed

The stock car racing world is about much more than speed. When I started researching this book, I knew little about the NASCAR nation. But after spending six months immersed in the NASCAR NEXTEL Cup Series, I learned my way around the sport. I experienced the unique atmosphere of the preeminent tracks—the grandeur of Daytona International Speedway in Florida, the history of Talladega Superspeedway in Alabama, the hominess of Pocono Raceway in Pennsylvania, the heat of California Speedway in Fontana. I also came to understand just how "big time" the sport is.

I had photographed plenty of other prime-time sporting events—the NBA Finals, the World Series, Super Bowls, and college bowl games—but at those games, I felt I was firmly rooted on the sidelines, looking in at the action. At a NASCAR race, I felt like I was inside the sport, especially at Talladega where I stayed in the infield all weekend. No matter where I was on the track, I felt immediately enveloped in the action, experiencing the cars' incredible speed, smelling the burning tires, hearing the deafening rumble of the motors.

In the hierarchy of the sport, the drivers are the superstars. They are at the pinnacle of what they do—negotiating turns fender-to-fender at 190 miles per hour, making split-second decisions that could cause a serious wreck or lead them to glory in Victory Lane. They receive the lion's share of the media and publicity spotlight, which has fueled the sport. (It is pretty funny to watch a winning driver do the baseball hat dance, quickly changing hats so that each sponsor gets a picture of its driver.)

Yet the faces of NASCAR go beyond the drivers. The fans, the crews, the drivers' families, the food vendors, and the track personnel all make up the backbone of this sport.

The focus and precision of the garage crews is particularly impressive. Usually between six or eight of them are working in the heat, noise, and time pressure of a small portable garage, trying to put the best car on the track come Sunday. They look like they are performing a tightly choreographed ballet. One guy goes low, another one goes high, and amazingly, they don't bump into each other amid the chains, pulleys, and motor lifts. The gearhead in me took a peak in their toolboxes and I was floored at how clean and well organized they were—not a speck of grease anywhere. Truly, there was a place for everything and everything was in its place. It inspired me to go home and reorganize my own garage.

The "over-the-wall" crew is made up of unbelievable athletes. Many fly in the morning of the race after practicing tire changes and gas fill-ups all week at their home bases. The tractor-trailer drivers who transport the cars are consummate professionals. They travel around the country like a circus, always magically managing to have the semis sparkling clean when they pull up to the track.

The fans are the heart of the sport, though. Most of the tracks offer an average of 100,000 seats, and the races are typically sellouts. The fans are passionate and committed. No one is a casual observer. They can all talk the talk, discussing cars, race history, and drivers' pedigrees. For a NASCAR fan, all that energy often lines up behind one driver.

The festival atmosphere of each race is a really good time, sometimes a little like Mardi Gras. Often the fans come to the same spot year after year and the races feel like a family holiday gathering. In one area is a millionaire row of $800,000 RVs with blow-up pools so fans can watch the laps poolside. Elsewhere, tent lots host die-hard fans camping from the back of their cars. No matter what their income level, everyone shares a common passion for the sport and is excited to witness the day's drama unfold on the track.

The races are full of hopes and dreams, especially among the newer, lesser-well-known drivers who are playing out a David versus Goliath story. These unknown drivers are doing the only thing they really want to do, but usually with a lot fewer resources than more established drivers. Even though their operations are somewhat ragtag, they all firmly believe that this is the race when they will break out.

Faces of NASCAR celebrates all of these people—the true essence of this sport—whether they are the top-skilled drivers, aspiring stars, dedicated crewmembers, or passionate fans. They all make NASCAR racing special—a sport built around family, teamwork, passion, and dedication.

The inherent beauty of the track and its atmosphere is also celebrated in this book. The combination of bright neon colors, sharp shadows, severe angles, and repeating patterns is striking. It also is a place where humor and irony can be found: four empty rocking chairs gathered near a sign promising a "garage vu," and a glowing food trailer offering "Tobacco" and "Snacks" like a beacon in the night.

Ultimately, this book is a portrait of what I saw during my six months in the NASCAR world. I hope you enjoy the ride.

— *Scott Robinson*

Drivers like Ryan Newman, Jamie McMurray, and Elliott Sadler are often seen as the face of racing. But even though they have the nerve to face turns at 180 miles an hour, they are only part of what makes racing great.

From rows of $800,000 RVs to fans camping out in the backs of their cars, no real NASCAR lover likes to miss the action on race day.

Crewmembers, whether they are crew chiefs like Jimmy Fennig or members of the garage or pit crew, are an essential part of a racing team's success.

Fans are the real heart of NASCAR racing. They turn every race into a festival, enjoying poolside seats and declaring their driver loyalties for all to see.

CHAPTER ONE

Family

Buffy Waltrip
One Big Family

Most people think of NASCAR as a league filled with intense competitors, but Buffy Waltrip thinks of it as an extended family.

"Every single weekend we see the same faces. Even though they're our competitors, they're our neighbors at night, they're our friends, they're our community. So there's comfort in that," she says. "Everyone wishes everyone good luck and good race, and we all say prayers. So it's really a special moment for the racing community that a lot of people probably don't realize."

The Waltrips—Buffy and husband Michael, a two-time Daytona 500 winner—have two daughters, Caitlin, 16, and Macy, 8, who make appearances on pit row if Mom thinks it will keep Dad's mind relaxed.

If she has pre-race jitters, she tries not to show it. "We don't have a lot of conversation," Buffy says about spending race mornings with Michael. "I don't ask him about the race car or how he thinks he's going to do. Enough people are asking him that. I've learned to just try to be there as a security blanket, so to speak, but not as a needy wife."

For the Waltrips, the races are often a social event where many family members and friends gather. Yet on race day, Buffy views her job as much more than being a social hostess. She is Michael's eyes and ears in the pits. The girls usually go back to the RV, where Macy might do homework with her nanny/tutor. But their mom can be found perched atop the pit box, focusing intently on the race.

"I sit on the pit box for several reasons," Buffy says. "One, Michael typically will ask me questions at the end of the race: What was it like in the pits today? Were the pit stops good? Did everybody work smoothly together? He doesn't really know the answer to because he's in the car.

"And if you're on the pit box and you've got your headset on, then nobody bothers you. I have found that if I'm here and I have friends and family here, it's more of a social event for them. I don't want them to think I'm very rude, but it's very difficult for me to socialize and be paying attention."

When I talked with the Waltrips, I reminded Buffy of the time I watched Michael wreck in Dover and the ghostly look on her face after the incident. Michael said he didn't really worry about getting hurt, but it was obvious that Buffy did, especially when I asked her if she is used to the risk her husband faces every time he climbs into his car.

"No, no," she says, adding that each time she sees a wreck, she gets a really sick feeling. "Part of the sick feeling goes away when you know your husband's okay," she says, but it never completely goes away because "unfortunately we have had a lot of tragedy in this sport."

Two-time Daytona 500 winner Michael Waltrip kisses his wife, Buffy, before a race at California Speedway. Buffy says her race day role is to be her husband's eyes and ears in the pits.

Dale Jr. (left) and Kerry Earnhardt (above) carry on the racing legacy their dad, Dale "The Intimidator" Earnhardt, built in the NASCAR NEXTEL Cup Series. "The Intimidator" not only won seven championship titles, but was the ultimate fan favorite.

Opposite page: The Eury family is a big part of the Earnhardts' success. Dale Earnhardt and Tony Eury, Earnhardt's longtime crew chief, married sisters, Brenda and Sandra Gee. From those marriages came Dale Jr. and Tony Jr. (pictured), cousins who have teamed to become a top racing team.

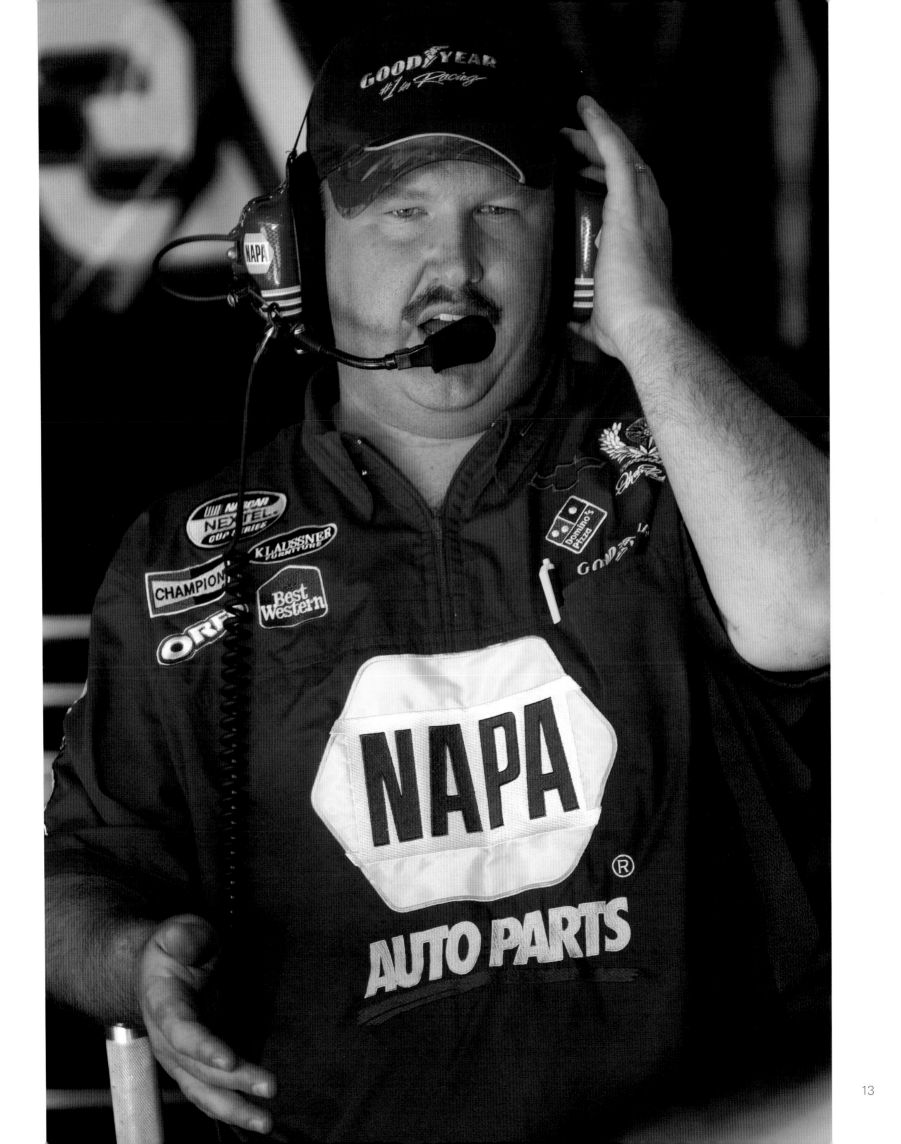

Richard Petty (opposite page), winner of a record 200 NASCAR NEXTEL Cup races, competed against his father, Lee, early on in his career. In fact, Lee disputed Richard's first victory, overturning the win to his favor. Richard's son, Kyle (above), also faced his dad, The King, in his early days on the NASCAR scene.

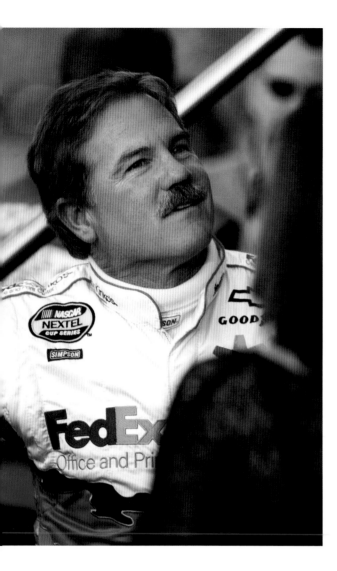

The Labonte brothers, Terry (above) and Bobby (right), are the only siblings to have both won a NASCAR NEXTEL Cup championship. Terry has won two titles in NASCAR's top series; Bobby has one NASCAR NEXTEL Cup title and a NASCAR Busch Series title.

NASCAR wouldn't exist if it weren't for Bill France Sr.,
who organized the sanctioning body and spearheaded
the building of Daytona International Speedway and
Talladega Superspeedway. His grandchildren,
Brian France, chairman and CEO of NASCAR, and
Lesa France Kennedy, president of International
Speedway Corporation, now play an integral part
in NASCAR's expanding popularity.

David and Austin Green
Racing's in the Genes

Five-year-old Austin Green seems destined for a life in NASCAR. You might say it's in the genes.

Austin, already driving karts, represents the next generation of a prominent NASCAR family that features three brothers: David, Mark, and Jeff Green. Austin's dad, David, the eldest, won the NASCAR Busch Series championship in 1994. Jeff, the youngest, won the NASCAR Busch Series championship in 2000, and now competes in the NASCAR NEXTEL Cup. Mark drove in the NASCAR Busch Series, too.

I've known about the Greens for years. We all grew up in Owensboro, Kentucky, where the Green boys were famous for racing karts as kids. (Owensboro is also the home of another famous NASCAR family—the Waltrips.) I remember the talk in the town, how the boys tuned their engines late at night, driving the neighbors crazy. But that was only natural; their dad drag raced as a hobby and took them along to the track.

"Racing was in our blood," David Green says. "The mere fact that we were going to the racetrack week in and week out embedded racing in our minds."

David picked up kart racing when he was 12 or 13, "which is kind of old nowadays," he says. By the time he was 20 or 21, he was running stock cars at the local track. During the day, he worked for his uncle, driving a concrete truck. At night, he worked on his race car. The other Green brothers followed the same path.

Sometimes the brothers competed against one another. "There were a few years when Jeff and I ran the [NASCAR] Busch Series together," David says. In 1996, all three brothers ran in the Busch Series. David says he and Jeff are the only two brothers to both be NASCAR Busch Series champions—an accomplishment that clearly gives the eldest Green brother a sense family pride.

"I always watch out for them," he adds, "and I look out for them and root 'em on."

Now, in his late 40s, David is thinking about driving for another year or two, then passing the torch to his son. Austin has been driving karts since he was four, and there's a good track in Charlotte, where the Greens live. The World Karting Association, which is the equivalent of NASCAR for karting, has a class for kids ages five through eight.

For now, Austin is only practicing, but it sounds like there's a good chance he'll be racing soon. His gratified father says this little boy "has made me proud several times," even as he confesses that it's hard to remember that Austin is only five years old.

"I've had a great career and I want to make sure Austin gets the same opportunity," David Green says. "I still think we can accomplish some things this year and next year, but I'm really kind of looking now to helping Austin move forward. If my nerves can handle it, it's going to be a lot of fun."

David Green (above) and his brothers (Jeff is on the opposite page) have all competed in the NASCAR Busch Series. David is nearing the end of his driving career and thinking about fostering his five-year-old son Austin's racing interests.

Kyle and Kurt Busch, part of NASCAR's growing under-30 driver crowd, are brothers who have both entered NASCAR's top racing series in the last five years.

Drivers often have their wives and children by their side during the introductions before each race. Above, Scott Riggs carries his son, Layne, on his shoulders before driver introductions at Dover.

Opposite page: John Hunter, Joe Nemechek's son, fits right in with his dad and the No. 01 Army team on race day.

Above: John Andretti, driver for Morgan-McClure Motorsports, at California. John is the nephew of Indy Car racing legend Mario Andretti and cousin to Michael Andretti. John drove in the NASCAR NEXTEL Cup Series for 10 years before turning to the NASCAR Busch Series full time.

Right: P. J. Jones, who has been racing in the NASCAR NEXTEL Cup Series since 1993, is the son of Parnelli Jones, a successful stock car and Indy Car racer. Parnelli won the 1963 Indianapolis 500 and was the owner of Al Unser Sr.'s cars in the 1970 and 1971 Indy 500 races.

Opposite page: Doug Yates—son of longtime car owner Robert Yates—holding his son, Christian, 5, at Talladega.

CHAPTER TWO

Teamwork

Driver Ricky Rudd and his crew chief Michael "Fatback" McSwain look at reports in the garage, trying to get the setup on the No. 21 Wood Brothers Ford ready for the UAW-GM Quality 500 at Lowe's Motor Speedway. Rudd finished ninth in the race.

Opposite page: Tony Glover, team manager for three teams at Ganassi Racing, talks with a crewmember at Talladega.

The Robert Yates No. 88 UPS Ford team coordinates a pit stop with tire change during the October 2005 UAW-Ford 500 race at Talladega.

Below: Crew chief Todd Parrott helps celebrate the No. 88 team's victory in the UAW-Ford 500 after driver Dale Jarrett captured the checkered flag.

Driver Joe Nemechek doesn't hesitate to help out his MB2 Motorsports team, picking up a broom to clean up the garage after the car blew a motor at Talladega.

Above: Tony Stewart often credits crew chief Greg Zipadelli with helping him stay focused to win the 2005 NASCAR NEXTEL Cup championship. The two have been a team since Tony's 1999 rookie season.

Right: The No. 20 Home Depot Chevrolet team working on the championship car at the Talladega garage.

34

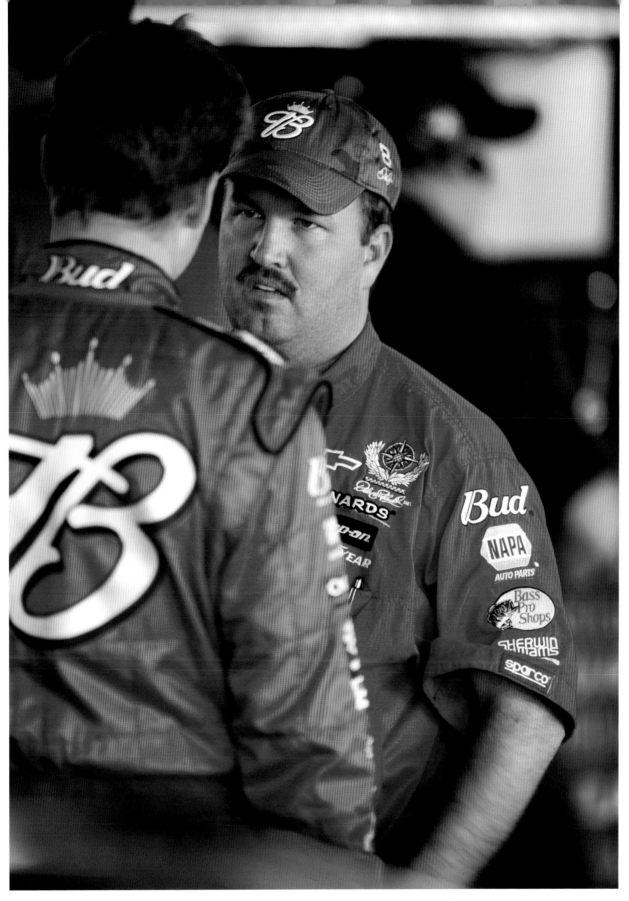

Crew chief Tony Eury Jr. talks with Dale Earnhardt Jr. in the garage area at Charlotte near the end of the 2005 season for the No. 8 Budweiser team.

Opposite page: Kurt Busch sits in a corner of the garage watching his team work on the No. 97 Roush Racing Ford at Lowe's Motor Speedway in 2005. Busch now drives for Penske Racing, in the No. 2 Miller Lite Dodge.

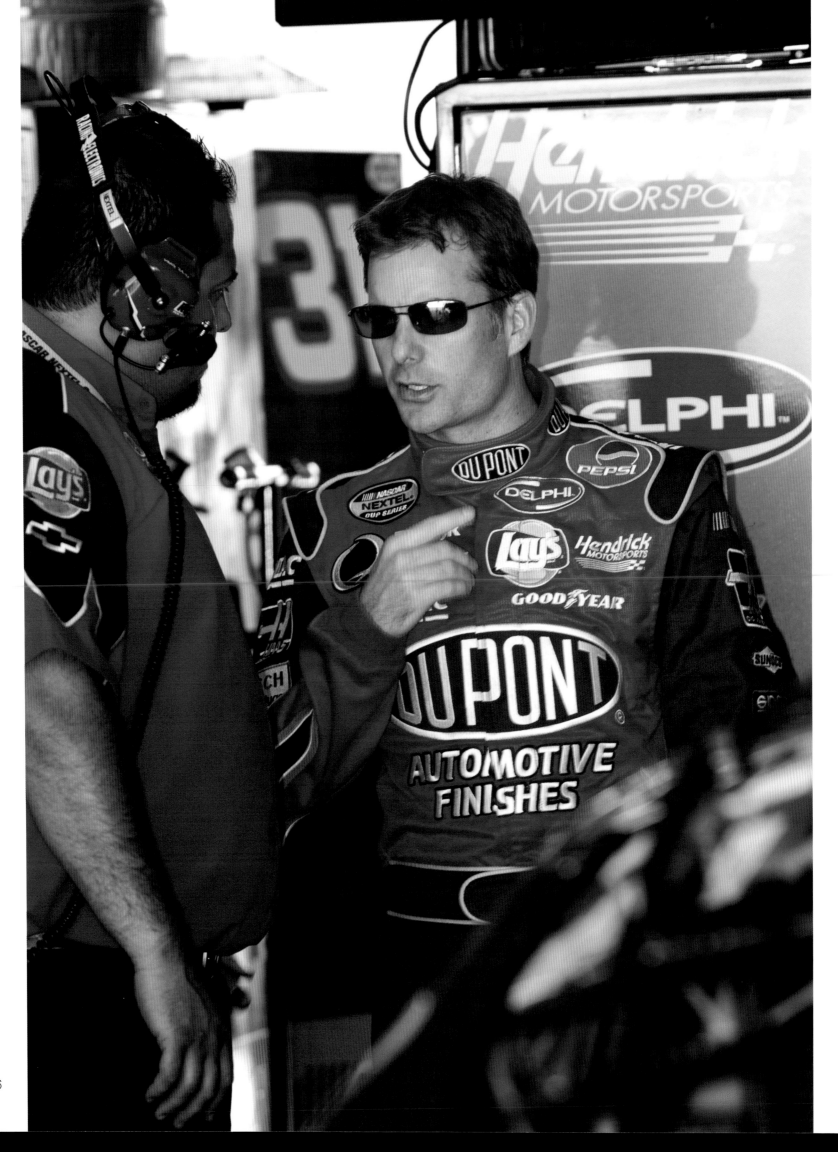

Getting the car ready for each race takes a lot of coordination between the driver and his team. On the opposite page, Jeff Gordon talks with a crewmember at Richmond, where the No. 24 DuPont Chevrolet finished 30th in the 2005 Chevy Rock & Roll 400. Above, Gordon shares a lighter moment with his new crew chief Steve Letarte at the 2006 Daytona 500.

Above: Car owner Ray Evernham talks over the setup of one of his cars at California. At right, he records notes for the Talladega UAW-Ford 500 showdown. Ray Everham owns the No. 19 car, driven by Jeremy Mayfield; the No. 9 car, driven by Kasey Kahne; and the No. 10 car, driven by Scott Riggs.

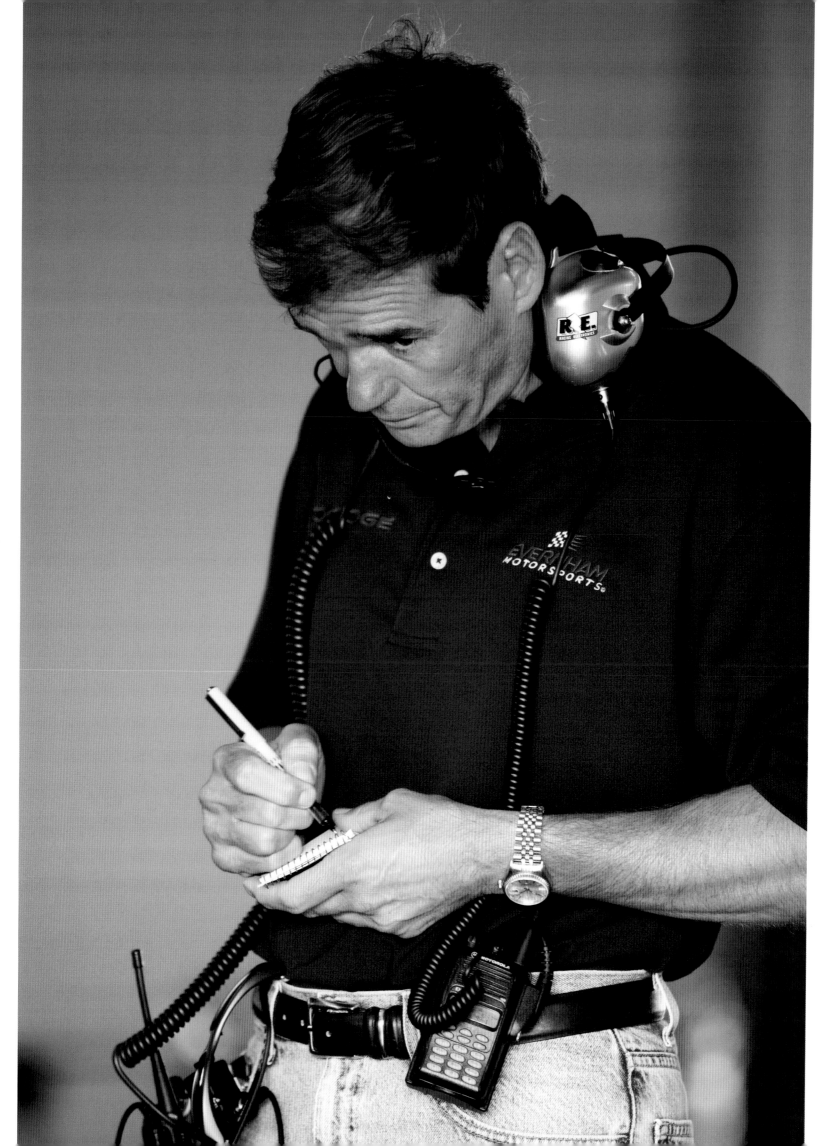

The No. 77 Kodak/Jasper Engines Dodge comes in for a pit stop at Talladega. With rookie Travis Kvapil at the wheel, the team recorded a 16th-place finish in the October 2005 race.

Casey Mears has a quick conference with crew chief Donnie Wingo before the start of the 2006 Daytona 500. Mears finished the 500 in second place.

Many racing observers believe legendary owner Jack Roush has found a new NASCAR superstar for his team in Carl Edwards, who finished his 2005 rookie NASCAR NEXTEL Cup season third in points.

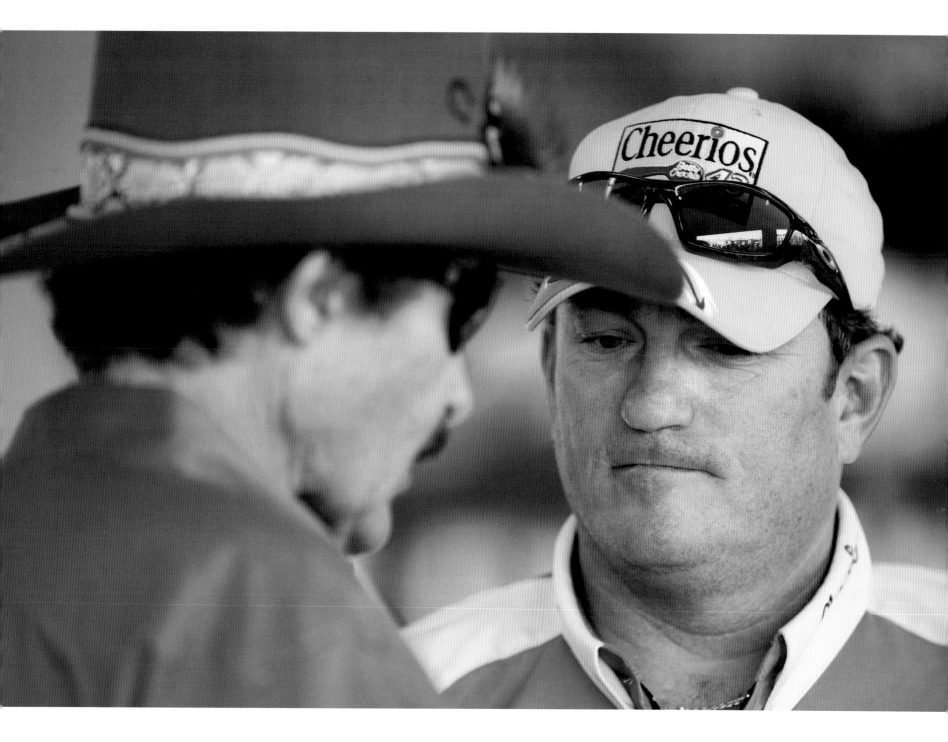

Crew chief Todd Parrott talks with owner Richard Petty at the beginning of the 2006 season at Daytona. Parrott moved from serving as Dale Jarrett's crew chief at the end of 2005 to become Bobby Labonte's right-hand man in 2006.

Owner Richard Childress stands atop the GM Goodwrench hauler watching his cars practice at Talladega. Childress was the first owner to win championships in the NASCAR NEXTEL Cup Series, the NASCAR Busch Series, and the NASCAR Craftsman Truck Series.

Chad Knaus has been Jimmie Johnson's crew chief since 2001. From 1993 to 1997, he was a part of Jeff Gordon's team at Hendrick Motorsports, serving as a general fabricator and manager of the chassis and body construction program.

Driver Mike Bliss (right), who started a personal record of 36 NASCAR NEXTEL Cup races in 2005, chats with a crewmember of the No. 0 NetZero Chevrolet team.

CHAPTER THREE
Determination

Stuart Kirby
Driving to Get a Full-Time Ride

For top NASCAR drivers, racing is a full-time job.

But for a young up-and-comer like Stuart Kirby, it's a chance to break out of an ordinary life. When he's not racing, he's home in Bowling Green, Kentucky, working for his dad at his family's funeral home business.

"I'm doing my apprenticeship to be a funeral director," Stuart says. "It's a few years' process. I assist with funeral directing, embalming, dealing with the families, and all the things going with it—delivering flowers, taking the casket to the cemetery."

If it sounds like Stuart Kirby is living two lives, he is. At 25, he's one of the younger drivers in the NASCAR league and is still searching for that steady ride. Like so many aspiring drivers, he started out racing karts as a little kid. In 2001, barely out of his teens, he made big headlines when he qualified in Charlotte right behind Jeff Gordon, now a four-time NASCAR NEXTEL Cup champion.

In 2005, Kirby qualified for seven NASCAR NEXTEL Cup races, finishing the season with a modest ranking of 54th. He's not discouraged, just determined to make it to the top.

I stumbled into Stuart's dad, Kevin Kirby, on a sweltering fall afternoon in Fontana, California. I was looking for some shade and found it right around the corner from the Kirby garage. Kevin and I began talking and quickly learned we were both Kentuckians; I went to college in Bowling Green, the Kirbys' hometown. I asked what he was doing at the race.

"My boy's racing the fifty-one car," he said.

While the hot drivers with names like Stewart, Gordon, and Earnhardt fly into town on private jets with dozens of team members and pit crews that are slick and polished, Stuart Kirby shows up with a team of just eight—a "rented crew," in his words, because he can't afford to hire a full-time support staff.

He says he's trying to soak up everything he can from the big-time drivers around him each time he's at the track.

"I met Gordon when I ran my first [NASCAR NEXTEL] Cup race in Charlotte," Kirby says. "The media was kind of making a big hype of me being twenty starting behind him, and him leading the championship. I went to introduce myself, told him I wasn't going to do anything aggressive or anything, 'cause I just wanted to get the race started. I think he really respected me coming up and talking to him, telling him I wasn't going to mess his day up. Every time he sees me now, he knows my name."

That first race didn't go so well, though. "We only got to run, like, fifty laps. I got caught up in a wreck," Kirby says. But he kept at it. And while he doesn't mind playing the role of new kid on the block, he knows that if he's ever going to break out of the family funeral business for good, he's got to be tough, as well as polite.

"You can't be too patient out there," Kirby says. "If somebody comes up and bumps you, you've got to show your going to bump him a little bit, and not give him any room."

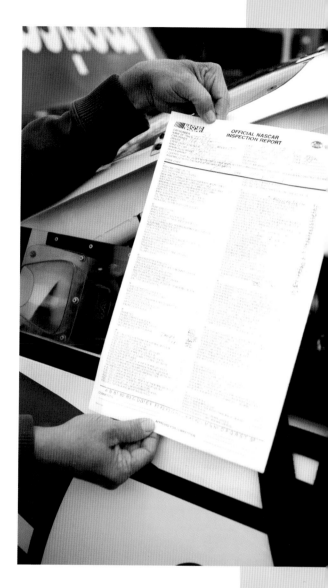

Here's a look at Stuart Kirby's NASCAR inspection sheet before the 2005 UAW-GM Quality 500 in Charlotte, where he finished 37th.

Stuart Kirby, driving the No. 51 car, has spent the last few years trying to get a full-time ride in NASCAR. He made headlines at Charlotte in 2001, when he qualified just behind NASCAR NEXTEL Cup champion Jeff Gordon.

In the noise of the Daytona Speedway, Jim Frinfrock watches for his team's car during the 2006 season-opening NASCAR Busch Series race.

Opposite page: Joe Gibbs, whose No. 20 car won the 2002 and 2005 NASCAR NEXTEL Cup championship, gets serious while preparing for the 2006 season-opening Daytona 500. Gibbs has not only orchestrated NASCAR title wins, but also coached three Super Bowl champion teams.

Longtime crew chief Jimmy Fennig shouts instructions to another team member while driver Kurt Busch (opposite page) gets ready behind the wheel at the 2005 UAW-Ford 500, where the No. 97 team finished eighth.

Jimmie Johnson has the eyes of a champion before practice at California, his hometown track. He won there in April 2002, in the NAPA Auto Parts 500.

Jeff Gordon holds the NASCAR NEXTEL Cup race record speed of 155.012 miles per hour at the California speedway.

Dale Earnhardt Jr. puts his helmet on before the UAW-GM Quality 500, where he finished 42nd in 2005.

Tim Jones spent 2005 as an engine tuner for Chip Ganassi Racing and now works for Joe Gibbs Racing.

Elliott Sadler had a breakout year in 2004, winning two NASCAR Nextel Cup races and earning eight top-5 finishes and fourteen top-10 finishes. In 2005, he added eight more top-5 finishes and twelve top-10 finishes to his career totals.

Ray Evernham went from crew chief to car owner in 1999, with the intent of leading Dodge back into NASCAR's elite series to field competitive teams. His team has already captured three wins in 2006.

Ken Howes, vice president of competition at Hendrick Motorsports, listening to team communications at Talladega. Hendrick's NASCAR NEXTEL Cup drivers are Kyle Busch, Jeff Gordon, Jimmie Johnson, and Brian Vickers.

Mark Nichols, the gas man on the No. 4 Lucas Oil Chevrolet car at Dover. The team finished 22nd at the September race in 2005.

Opposite page: Brian Vickers ready to take on the competition at Pocono, where he placed 14th in the Pennsylvania 500 in 2005.

Jack Roush began his NASCAR team around No. 6 driver Mark Martin, who plans to leave NASCAR NEXTEL Cup racing to run Craftsman trucks full time in 2007.

Jimmy Makar, senior vice president of Joe Gibbs Racing, in the team's pit box.

Doug Yates, an engine builder who oversees operations at Roush-Yates Racing Engines, times a car during practice at Talladega.

Left: Darren Russell, a crewmember for Evernham Motorsports. The organization that was founded in 1999 now has more than 250 employees.

Previous pages: Kasey Kahne and 2005 NASCAR NEXTEL Cup champion Tony Stewart talk shop before the fall race at Talladega, where Stewart finished second and Kahne finished 13th.

Greg Biffle, who has twice finished second in the NASCAR NEXTEL Cup points race, was the first driver to win championships in both the NASCAR Craftsman Truck Series and Busch Series before moving full time to Cup racing in 2003.

Opposite page: In 2006, Scott Riggs, driver for the No. 10 Valvoline Dodge, hopes to rebound from a disappointing 2005 season and a DNQ in the 2006 opener at Daytona. He switched teams—from MB2 Racing to Evernham Motorsports— between seasons.

Kevin Buskirk served as the interim crew chief for Elliott Sadler and the No. 38 M&M's Ford for the final nine races in 2005.

Opposite page: Jeff Gordon has always been known as a driver with intense focus and determination. Both traits have helped him win 73 victories in 14 NASCAR NEXTEL Cup seasons.

For 2006, Bobby Labonte moved from driving the Joe Gibbs Racing No. 18 Interstate Batteries Chevrolet to Richard Petty Enterprises, where he's behind the wheel of the legendary No. 43 car.

Dale Jarrett, driver of the No. 88 UPS Ford, is a veteran stock car champion who hopes to beat some of the new drivers and make the Chase for the NASCAR NEXTEL Cup in 2006. Jarrett has been a NASCAR contender for over 20 years.

Team owner Richard Childress' determination to win made an impact early on in 2006, when driver Jeff Burton won the pole for the Daytona 500 and won the NASCAR Busch Series race at Atlanta in March.

Opposite page: In 1998, Matt Kenseth's first full season in the NASCAR Busch Series, he won three races and finished second in points. Since then, he has posted 15 wins in the series.

Kevin Harvick, who was selected to drive the GM Goodwrench car after Dale Earnhardt in 2001, has never made it a secret that he is determined to find success behind the wheel of the renumbered No. 29 car.

Left: T. J. Bell is a part-time NASCAR Busch Series driver. In 2005, he started eight races, including the Ameriquest 300 at California, where he drove the Heathcliff's Cat Litter Chevrolet to a 38th-place finish.

Opposite page: This is what every top driver perseveres 36 racing events to win: the NASCAR NEXTEL Cup championship trophy.

CHAPTER FOUR
Fan Fervor

Ben and Kegan Sanders
Growing up NASCAR Fans

Some little boys worship baseball and football. The Sanders boys—Ben, 10, and Kegan, 6—worship NASCAR.

At home in Wichita, Kansas, the bedroom these brothers share is a shrine to America's fastest growing sport. The shelves are stuffed with dozens of Hot Wheels cars, die-cast race cars, and haulers—anything that has a NASCAR connection—and there are even more cars in the toy box. The walls are covered with NASCAR posters. NASCAR pennants and checkered NASCAR NEXTEL Cup flags hang from the ceiling and double as curtains. Even the sheets have a NASCAR motif.

But the biggest NASCAR trinket of all—the best memento a little boy who loves racing could hope for—is a tire from Jeff Gordon's car, with the colored-chalk number 24 still visible on the rubber. It's Ben Sanders' prize catch from a storybook weekend in October 2005, when he celebrated his 10th birthday at the Talladega track.

It was a long drive, nearly 1,000 miles, but well worth it for these two little boys, who have been raised on NASCAR. Their mom, Kristi, a homemaker and bookkeeper, and their dad, Brent, the chief of maintenance for Lear Jet, have been fans since before the boys were born. There's a flagpole in front of the Sanders house in Wichita, and neighbors always know when it's a race day because a NASCAR NEXTEL Cup flag will be flying high and proud.

The boys don't agree on who's the best driver, though. Kegan is a Tony Stewart fan, probably because he likes going to Home Depot, Stewart's sponsor, with his dad. He even has a hat autographed by the 2005 NASCAR NEXTEL Cup champion. "Kegan chased him all around, yelling 'Tony! Tony!'" mom Kristi says. Stewart, unable to resist the sight of such an eager, fresh-faced six-year-old, stopped to sign.

But big brother Ben is a devoted Jeff Gordon fan. He got that from his mom.

"I just like the way he races," Kristi explains. "He's very talented and he has good sportsmanship. He's the only one who ever gave Dale Earnhardt, and now Dale Jr., a challenge."

So on race day, October 2, Ben's birthday, the Sanders brothers were in the infield, peering behind a chain-link fence into the garage area, craning their necks for just a teensy glimpse of the drivers who are their heroes. That's when Brent sprang into action, sweet-talking Gordon's crew into giving up a tire. It didn't take much; he told a tire man it was Ben's birthday and the tire was all theirs.

As it turned out, it was a rough day for Jeff Gordon. "He tried to go around and he ended up slamming into the wall," Ben remembers, "so he missed out on that race."

That didn't scare Ben. He already knows what he wants to be when he grows up: a NASCAR driver, of course.

Did you have any doubt?

Ben peers through the fences at Talladega with brother Kegan (left). The boys and their parents made a 1,000-mile trek from Wichita, Kansas, to see the October 2 race for Ben's 10th birthday.

Ben Sanders, 10, sports the colors of his favorite driver, Jeff Gordon. He likes Gordon because his mom, another avid NASCAR fan, rallies behind the four-time NASCAR champ.

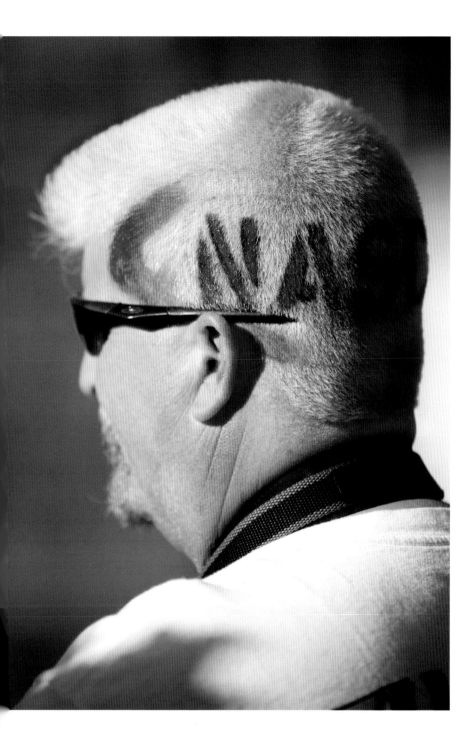

Jim Long of Ellicott City, Maryland, airbrushed a NASCAR motif into his hair before the Great American Race at Daytona.

Tony Stewart fan Dory Richardson of Myrtle Beach, South Carolina, takes a snooze in the infield after a race at Talladega.

Opposite page: Don Griffin of Jacksonville, Florida, shows off his driver No. 8 pride at the season-opening race at Daytona, where Dale Junior has shown his ability to work the draft in restrictor-plate racing and win.

Fans in the infield at Talladega watch the race action on the big screen, rather than the on track.

Robert Thorne and Darlene Boyden, both of New Jersey, enjoy a day in the infield at Pocono. Pocono is a 2.5-mile tri-oval and hosted its first NASCAR NEXTEL Cup race in 1974.

Robert Bustos Jr.
The Hatman

Meet the Hatman.

He is Robert Bustos Jr., a 45-year-old maintenance worker in Salinas, California. Weekdays, Bustos keeps busy with his job at his local school district. But on nights and weekends, this crazy and creative racing fan with an inventor's touch and an eye for self-promotion is transformed into . . . the Hatman.

I first spied the Hatman along pit row at California Motor Speedway, where he stood out from the thousands of fans clamoring for a view of the cars. I could tell he had been photographed a lot—he seemed like a real pro—and I asked him to tell me his story.

It's a family tale, like many NASCAR stories, and it all started about 15 years ago when Robert and his younger brother, Cesar, an electrician, were bitten by the NASCAR bug. "We used to sit there and watch the races, and my brother would say, 'Wouldn't that be neat, to be a pit crewmember?'" Robert remembers.

That dream eventually became a reality for Cesar. When he helped wire a new garage for Carroll Racing, he landed a full-time job in racing, moving to Alabama and eventually Charlotte, where he now works for Penske Racing in the body and paint department. In 1998, Cesar came home to California for Christmas and found his big brother tinkering with a miniature pit crew he had been making for a display case.

Robert remembers the conversation well. "I said 'Hey Cheese—I would call him Cheese because his name is Cesar—what would you think if I put this on a hat? He says, 'Robert, do it. They'll put you in magazines; you'll get on TV.'"

The hat features a pit crew, driver, and car, with an engine that really revs, all hand-painted and set in perfect miniature atop a hardhat on Robert Bustos' head. So how does it work? Robert will give some details, but not all. Clark Kent never told how he became Superman, so why should Robert Bustos tell how he became the Hatman?

"I went to toy stores, stores everywhere in town, just to look for little guys that would be close enough to a pit crew. But I'm not going to say what they used to be," he says. "I built my own headsets; they were like rubber grommets with a wire, like a spring, that went down to a battery pack. I found these cars that would start up. Then I rigged that up to a little switch so I could just hit this button, and the whole car moves."

The Hatman made his NASCAR debut in 1999 at Talladega, where Robert boasts he got "more air time than my brother's race car." Soon, he was referring to himself in the third person as the Hatman. Two years ago at Fontana, he spotted a movie production underway. "I go, 'The Hatman's gotta go over there. They might put me in it.'"

He says the producers did for a fast three seconds, but hey, who said fame isn't fleeting? Last year, the Hatman says he scored really big when he says he was voted the "Number One NASCAR Fan" during a Speed TV NASCAR special.

Now that he's achieved fame, the Hatman has his eyes on fortune.

"My ultimate goal," he says, "is to find a sponsor to help me patent this. That's my dream."

Robert "The Hatman" Bustos Jr. constructed his elaborate pit stop hat himself, scouring stores for the little figures that could double as crewmembers.

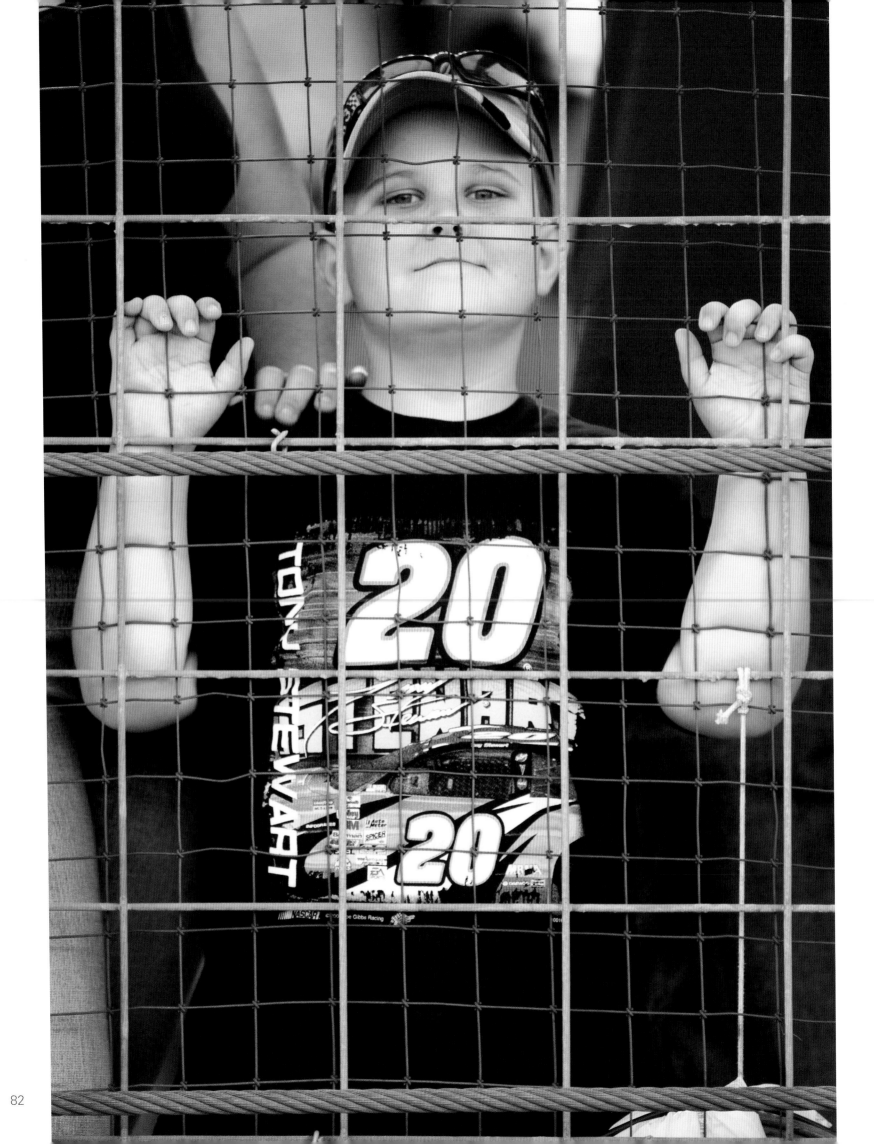

Opposite page: A young, enthusiastic Tony Stewart fan watches through the fence at Lowe's Motor Speedway so he can catch a glimpse of his hero during driver's introductions. Stewart finished 25th there at the 2005 UAW-GM Quality 500.

Right and below: Fans of all ages enjoy the race from the infield at Dover.

Scott and Corinne Schoenich won tickets to a Dover race as part of a nationwide contest sponsored by Sunoco. They bought their matching Ryan Newman No. 12 ALLTEL Dodge pants when they discovered they couldn't go in the garage area wearing shorts.

Opposite page: A pair of NASCAR fans raise Old Glory on their RV before the Talladega race.

During race weekends, many fans dream of getting a photo of their favorite car. Of course, the No. 8 Budweiser Chevrolet is one that instantly draws a crowd.

Lisa Smith
A Dream Meeting

Many female fans line up each race weekend to get Dale Jr.'s autograph on just about anything, especially die cast No. 8 cars.

Lisa Smith is just one of the legions of dedicated Dale Earnhardt Jr. fans. Her devotion goes so far that she has two tattoos celebrating her favorite driver.

Like NASCAR fans everywhere, Lisa Smith has big dreams. "I would love to just try to meet him, to sit down and talk to him," she says. "That would be awesome, just a one-on-one talk."

The "him" in Smith's NASCAR fan fantasy is Dale Earnhardt Jr., and she has come closer to realizing the dream than most. Once, at an event in Winston-Salem, she persuaded an Earnhardt sponsor to take her to the pressroom to meet her favorite driver. She cornered Junior in the elevator and got him to autograph her suede Budweiser jacket. Another time, she won a radio "Meet and Greet Dale Jr." contest after hitting the redial button on her phone hundreds of times.

"We all sat at barstools, and he sat at a table and answered questions," she says. The only problem was that she was too nervous to speak.

At 42, Smith, a doctor's receptionist in Durham, North Carolina, fancies herself the ultimate Dale Jr. fan. She first followed his father's career. She was watching the Daytona 500 on television in 2001, the day Dale Earnhardt died; she cried so hard she couldn't go to work the next day.

Now she's all Junior, all the time. She even sports two Dale Jr. tattoos, one on her lower back and one on her shoulder for all to see. The one on her shoulder is patterned after a Dale Jr. bracelet she bought at a NASCAR store.

"I wish it was summer here all the time so you could see it all [the time]," she says. "I can't explain it. I guess I want to show people how much I support him and no matter what, when he has a good day or a bad day, that he is my driver."

While she watched NASCAR races on television for years with her father, Smith has only recently been attending them. That began when a lawyer who is a patient of the doctor she works for spotted her Dale Jr. paraphernalia in the office.

"He asked me about the races and I told him I didn't have the money to spend to go," she said. "He gave me tickets to Charlotte, and he has given me tickets to every race around here. He takes me in his little NASCAR party van, and we all go."

Smith knows that every fan thinks they're the best fan out there, but she *really* thinks she's the best. She wonders what it would be like to have a "one-on-one dinner, to get to know the real Dale Jr." But when it comes to the ultimate Dale Jr./Lisa Smith fantasy, her lips are sealed.

"I'm not going to answer that!"

Opposite page: Fans lucky enough to secure garage passes get an up-close-and-personal look at their favorite cars undergoing final mechanical adjustments and inspection. Some even take guided tours of the garage area.

A tour guide gives fans an inside look at the garage area at Lowe's Motor Speedway.

A fan gets his chance to see how well his lug nut tightening skills match up against the pros as part of the pre-race festivities at Dover.

A fan, decked out with a colorful NASCAR hat, watches the garage area at California Speedway. Before the track was built, the land was home to Kaiser Steel Mill, the first steel mill west of the Rocky Mountains.

Fans enjoy an evening at a makeshift old-fashioned saloon after the race at Talladega.

A fan signs the finish line at
the Fontana, California, track,
which hosted its first race in 1997.

CHAPTER FIVE
Legends

Richard Petty
A Winning Belt Buckle

When I began work on *Faces of NASCAR*, there was one person I knew I had to meet: the legendary Richard Petty, winner of an unbelievable 200 NASCAR NEXTEL Cup races. My first encounter with Petty came more than two decades ago, in 1984, when I was working as a newspaper photographer for the *Florida Times-Union* in Jacksonville. I had been assigned to cover the big July race at Daytona. It was my first NASCAR race, and I thought the place to be was down low, in Turn One.

None of the other photographers were in that spot, which I thought was a little unusual. A few minutes into the race, I learned why: as the cars blew by me at full speed, I was showered with bits of rubber and road debris, making the unbearable heat all the more unbearable and the picture-taking impossible. I made a sheepish retreat to higher ground, hoping the other shooters weren't laughing too hard at the rookie.

King Richard won that race—having already racked up seven Daytona 500 crowns—and his victory lap is seared in my memory. He drove the No. 43 Buick Regal to the middle of the track, stopped the car and—showing no signs of exhaustion after that grueling race—hiked up the steep bank of the Daytona Speedway to shake the hand of President Ronald Reagan.

So, 21 years later, when I arrived at Pocono for the first of a series of races I would photograph for *Faces of NASCAR*, I was hoping to see Petty again. It didn't take long. I was setting up for a photo shoot with Kyle Busch at the No. 5 garage when a tall, thin man with a black cowboy hat zoomed by on foot. Petty moves fast, even when he's not behind the wheel of a car. By the time I realized who it was, he was four garages away, and I was unable to desert my post.

My next good Petty sighting came in Richmond. Petty had traded in his black cowboy hat for a white one, and I photographed him sitting atop a cooler, sporting dark sunglasses and flashing his trademark 1,000-watt smile. When I was reviewing my images, the detail in Petty's belt buckle caught my eye. When I looked at the frame under high magnification, I knew what I wanted to photograph next.

Most people think a portrait can be only a picture of a person's face, but I often think small details can tell as much or more about a person. To me, King Richard's belt buckle and the casual, yet confident way he loops his thumbs in his jeans pockets say everything you need to know about the seven-time NASCAR champ. I shot the photo above in Dover. The shoot lasted all of about three minutes, and I wanted just one more chance to meet up with The King.

My moment came in Charlotte. I brought two 11x14-inch prints of the belt buckle photograph with me and awkwardly carted them around all weekend, looking for any chance to get them signed.

Finally, I spotted him, in front of the Petty hauler, right where you'd expect him to be. There I was, standing in line with a bunch of other fans, wanting to get something signed. I patiently waited my turn, and when it came, I reminded King Richard of our brief time together in Dover. We laughed, and he signed his name with a flourish.

In another three minutes, I was gone.

Richard Petty, one of NASCAR's most legendary drivers, is known for his trademark cowboy hat, sunglasses, smile, and championship belt buckle.

Many of Dale Earnhardt's ardent fans now cheer for his son, Dale Earnhardt Jr., as he carries on his father's racing legacy.

Opposite page: Dale Earnhardt will always be one of NASCAR's greatest legends. After his death at the 2001 Daytona 500, a commemorative statue of Dale was placed at the Daytona racetrack.

After 25 years, Rusty Wallace has retired from spending every race Sunday behind the wheel, but he's still involved in the NASCAR scene. He will report on 20 NASCAR races for ESPN's *SportsCenter* in 2006.

Above and right: Jack Roush was an outsider to stock car racing when he first decided to become a NASCAR owner. But now Roush is a familiar face (and hat) on pit row and he backs five of the sport's top drivers and cars, all of which made the 2005 Chase for the NASCAR NEXTEL Cup.

Opposite page: Mark Martin, who has come heartbreakingly close to winning a NASCAR NEXTEL Cup championship four times, extended his tenure in the top-tier stock racing field to get one more shot at the trophy in 2006.

Car owner and engine builder Robert Yates (who stands with driver Dale Jarrett after the team's Talladega win) has been involved in the world of NASCAR racing since 1968, when he joined the legendary Holman-Moody team as air gauge department manager.

Robert Yates Racing driver Dale Jarrett followed in his father's footsteps when he first started competing in the Limited Sportsman Division of stock car racing. His NASCAR NEXTEL Cup accomplishments include winning 32 races, including the 1993 Daytona 500, and securing the 1999 championship trophy.

At 64 years old, Morgan Shepherd is one of the oldest drivers to regularly compete in both the NASCAR NEXTEL Cup Series and NASCAR Busch Series. He has won four NASCAR NEXTEL Cup races in his 26-year career and racked up 63 top-5s and 168 top-10s.

Opposite page: Michael Waltrip etched his place in racing history on one of its darkest days, when he won the 2001 Daytona 500 on the same day Dale Earnhardt lost his life after a late-race accident at the track.

Bill Elliott has been in NASCAR garages since the days drivers helped cut up car bodies right alongside crewmembers. He entered his first NASCAR NEXTEL Cup race in 1976, when he was just 20 years old.

Bobby Labonte didn't start racing in NASCAR's Busch Series until 1990, after he had spent years winning on short tracks. He moved up to compete in the NASCAR NEXTEL Cup Series in 1993 and won a championship title there just six years later.

Jimmy Fennig started his legendary crew chief career in the ASA, working with Mark Martin (with whom he later reteamed with in NASCAR). He has also served as crew chief for many of racing's top drivers, including Bobby Allison, Kurt Busch, and Jamie McMurray.

CHAPTER SIX
Good Times

Denny Hamlin, one of the 2006 NASCAR NEXTEL Cup rookies, shares in the star-studded affair that is the Daytona 500, talking trackside with rock musician Kid Rock.

Opposite page: While meeting with fans can sometimes get overwhelming for drivers, it's still a race day highlight. Here champion Tony Stewart shares a laugh with a young fan at Richmond.

Jimmy Elledge, the 2005 crew chief for the No. 41 car driven by Casey Mears, has a good laugh in the garage at Lowe's Motor Speedway. Before joining Chip Ganassi Racing, Elledge worked with drivers Kenny Wallace, Bobby Hamilton, and Dale Jarrett.

Opposite page: Matt Kenseth and Dale Earnhardt Jr. have been friends since the days they were both driving in the NASCAR Busch Series. They battled each other for the 2000 NASCAR NEXTEL Cup Raybestos Rookie of the Year title, which Kenseth won.

Kasey Kahne, one of NASCAR's most popular drivers among women, flashes a million-dollar smile before a NASCAR Busch Series race at Richmond.

Opposite page: Dale Earnhardt Jr. sneaks a smile before having a tough day on the Richmond track, where he finished 42nd in October 2005.

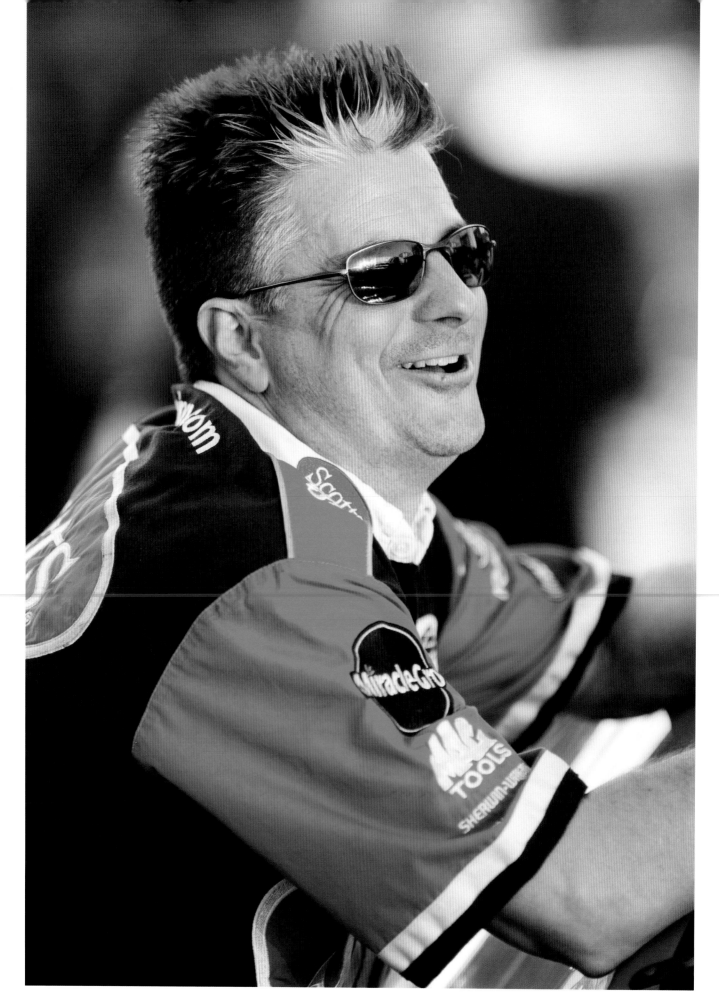

Pierre Kuettel, the 2005 car chief for the Roush Racing No. 99 car, dyed his hair to match the team colors at Charlotte.

Jamie McMurray, who is driving for Roush Racing in 2006, shows his excitement for the race ahead at Dover. He finished 13th there in both 2005 races.

Elliott Sadler jokes with Mark Martin and Carl Edwards before driver introductions at the Emerson Radio 250 NASCAR Busch Series race at Richmond. Sadler finished sixth in the race.

Kenny Wallace chats with another driver before introductions at the Richmond NASCAR Busch Series race.

A smiling Richard Childress gets ready to sign autographs for fans at Talladega. Childress' team includes 2006 Cup rookie Clint Bowyer, Jeff Burton, and Kevin Harvick.

Team owner Joe Gibbs smiles about a come-from-behind fifth-place finish by driver Tony Stewart in the 2006 Daytona 500.

Darrell Waltrip shares a lighter moment with fans as he stands next to his team's truck. Waltrip rebuilt his NASCAR Craftsman Truck team in 2004 and his driver David Reutimann was named the series' top rookie that year.

Jeremy Mayfield, driver of the No. 19 Ray Evernham Dodge, at Richmond, where in 2005 he finished 13th and 6th, respectively.

Opposite page: Darren Russell, crewmember for the No. 9 car, has a laugh in the garage area before his team and driver Kasey Kahne record a sixth-place finish at California in September 2005.

The No. 88 UPS team's crew chief Todd Parrott talks with a teammate at Talladega, where the car driven by Dale Jarrett captured the checkered flag.

NASCAR NEXTEL Cup and NASCAR Busch Series driver Mike Wallace hangs out in front of the hauler at Lowe's Motor Speedway. Before driving in NASCAR events, he won more than 300 short-track races during the 1970s and 1980s.

Carl Edwards had something to smile about after winning the pole in California in September 2005. The former subsitute teacher won four NASCAR NEXTEL Cup races in his first season in the series.

After serving part of the 2005 season as Michael Waltrip's crew chief, Tony Eury Jr. reunited with Dale Earnhart Jr. for the last nine races of the season.

Scott Wimmer first got behind the wheel of ATVs at the age of eight. He began his auto racing career at just 14 and finished his first full-time season in the NASCAR Busch Series in 2001, when he was 25.

Jeff Gordon's crew chief Steve Letarte, ready for the racing year ahead at the 2006 Daytona opener. He has been with Hendrick Motorsports for 12 years, where he first worked as a tire specialist and mechanic.

CHAPTER SEVEN

Race Day

Kirk Butterfield
Relying on Instincts

Squinting into the distance, Kirk Butterfield looked lost in thought as he leaned over a steel equipment case outside the First Interstate Battery garage, where he worked as an engine tuner for Bobby Labonte in 2005 and now tunes for rookie J.J. Yeley.

His forearms were protected by Kevlar sleeves, essential for sticking your hand into a hot motor to pull a spark plug and replace it in short order. His ears were glued to a radio headset as he listened intently to the conversation between Labonte and the crew chief—a talk that would provide Butterfield critical clues about how the car was running that day at Dover and how he could make it perform even better in time for race day.

At 40, Butterfield is a rare breed among modern NASCAR mechanics. He doesn't just use computers or newfangled technology to diagnose engine problems. He also relies on his instincts and his senses—plus years of experience working with some of the biggest names in auto racing—to see what has to be done.

"You look down inside the plug toward the base of the porcelain for the fuel ring. That will tell you if the car is running rich or lean," he says, describing how he makes his engine adjustments. "When you can't hardly see the fuel ring, it's lean. Then the porcelain itself will tell you how the timing is. If it has a little glaze to it, then the timing is perfect. But if it has a little pepper effect, then you've got too much timing and it's running hot."

Butterfield knows that the tiniest adjustments can make the difference between winning and losing a race. It's something that's been ingrained in him since he was a kid, growing up in Carrollton, Ohio, with a father who has worked as a Chevrolet mechanic for four decades. When Butterfield was just eight, he and his father restored a 1923 roadster, replacing its ancient motor with one from a 1966 Corvette.

"It was just the excitement of the cars and building on the engines and hearing them running, the satisfaction of doing everything with your two hands," he says about his early engine-building interests. "From then on, I was always hooked on cars."

So hooked that he bought his first one—a 1955 Chevy two-door 210 sedan—when he was just 13 and not even old enough to drive. "I still have it to this day," Butterfield says. "I bought it with thirty-thousand original miles and the only thing I've really done to it is build a small-block Chevy, and I have a supercharger on it. I've showed it quite a bit, driven it everywhere."

At the track, Butterfield must be prepared to work fast. In a pinch, he can take an engine out of a car and drop in new one in 40 minutes flat. But he's modest about his work, insisting he doesn't do it all on his own.

"It's just not one guy," Butterfield says. "Everybody has to work together, no matter if you're replacing an engine in forty minutes or getting a car ready for a weekend of racing. It's a team sport."

Opposite page: Kirk Butterfield, now J.J. Yeley's engine man, uses years of experience and instincts to diagnose engine problems, rather than just technical information gleaned from a computer.

Darren Russell, crewmember for the No. 9 Ray Evernham Dodge, isn't afraid to get his hands dirty on race day.

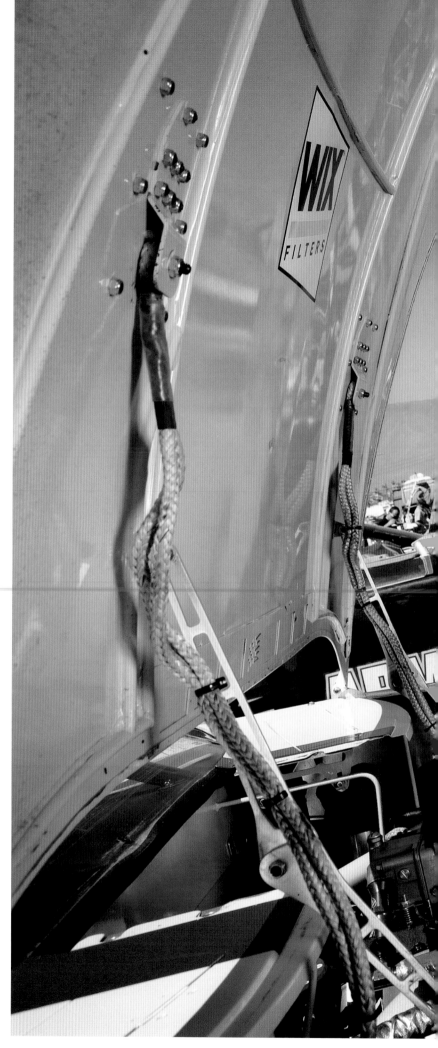

Car owner and engine expert Jack Roush inspects some spark plugs before the 2005 September race at Dover, where longtime Roush driver Mark Martin finished fourth.

Crew chief Greg Zipadelli leans in to talk with driver Tony Stewart before a race at Lowe's Motor Speedway. He has been working with Stewart since 1999 and is a modern-day crew chief, handling the roles of mechanic, coach, and visionary.

Opposite page: One of the crewmembers for the No. 32 PPI Racing Chevrolet repairs damage to the car so it can get back out on the Dover track. In the 2005 MBNA RacePoints 400, Bobby Hamilton Jr. drove the car to a 33rd-place finish.

Tony Stewart talks with Rusty Wallace during a slow moment in the garage at Dover, before the 2005 MBNA RacePoints 400 where Wallace finished 3rd and Stewart came in 18th.

Opposite page: A crewmember hangs out of the No. 19 Ray Evernham Dodge while he completes some final adjustments at Dover.

Wes Adams, a crewmember for the No. 31 Cingular car, practices the waiting game during some downtime at California. Adams is an engine tuner for Richard Childress Racing.

Scotty Hazlett, a former mechanic for MB2 Motorsports, watches practice at Dover.

Each team brings a number of tires to the race and usually one crewmember is in charge of recording all the tire specifications and wear. This information will help calculate how long the car can run with a particular set of tires.

Opposite page: Lisa Smokstad, one of the few female pit crewmembers in NASCAR, uses her talents as a tire specialist for the Rick Hendrick No. 25 car. She has worked in auto racing for 12 years, first working on her brother-in-law's car. She is also a gymnastics coach.

Glenn Wheeler
Tires Are Like Snowflakes

A closeup look at some typical NASCAR tire markings. These are for the No.1 Army car at the fall 2005 Dover race.

Glenn Wheeler's job is where the rubber hits the road.

As a tire specialist for Robby Gordon's crew, 20-year-old Wheeler is one of the countless anonymous, behind-the-scenes people who can make or break a driver's race. His job is to know everything there is to know about tires, and it's a lot more complicated than increasing and decreasing air pressure.

Tires, according to Wheeler, are like snowflakes: no two are alike. Each one comes with its own detailed biography, courtesy of Goodyear, the official tire manufacturer for NASCAR. The bios are chock full of critical details, like when and where the tire was made, the compound of its rubber, the curing press used in its manufacture, and the all-important "spring rating," which measures the stiffness of the sidewall.

Gordon's team goes through roughly 10 sets of tires, 40 tires in all, during any given race. It's up to Wheeler to comb through all the information and match those tires as closely as possible, arranging them in a series of perfect quartets. But, unlike regular car tires, four racing tires are not always the same size.

"The right side tires are usually about an inch and three quarters bigger than the left side," Wheeler explains, noting the difference is what tire specialists call stagger. "It just helps the car naturally want to make a turn."

Wheeler was the first person I met at my first NASCAR race for this book, at Pocono in 2005. He struck me as smart and enthusiastic, and I liked him immediately. Robby Gordon must have too, because he hired Wheeler when he was still in high school in Orange County, California. Wheeler had been working for a machinist, who asked him to deliver something to the Gordon shop. As luck would have it, Gordon was there.

"I said, 'Hey, I'd like to work on race cars, and this is where I would like to be,'" Wheeler says. "And he pretty much said, 'All right, you start Monday.'"

Wheeler started with odd jobs—sweeping out the garage, running parts, staying late at night to learn the ins and outs of tires and mechanics. He was promoted to tire specialist as soon as he graduated. Two seasons later, he still sometimes gets butterflies in his stomach on race days.

"It's the day I've got to perform just as much as the guys that are going over the wall," Wheeler says. "Say I've got ten sets, I've got forty different tires that I've got to look after, and then I've got all kinds of information that I've got to record and relay to the crew chief making decisions. A lot of those decisions come off the tires, so it can get pretty stressful. But it's also pretty cool when you see your car going by, passing someone at one-hundred-eighty, one-hundred-ninety miles per hour."

One of Wheeler's most stressful moments in 2005 came during the Charlotte race in October, when it seemed as if every driver was having tire blowouts. Wheeler knew going into the race that there might be trouble because the track had recently been resurfaced. But no one could predict how out-of-control things would get until cars started hitting the wall.

"That night I was scared," Wheeler says. "I wasn't scared of getting fired. I wasn't scared of running out of tires. I was scared for Robby, my friend, that a tire would go down and put him in the wall."

Gordon did have some tire troubles in Lap Two, but not the kind of tire damage that eliminated 15 cars from the race. "It was bad," Wheeler says. "And I don't think anybody's to blame; it's just something that happened."

Opposite page: Glen Wheeler, driver Robby Gordon's tire specialist, says tires are like snowflakes: no two are alike.

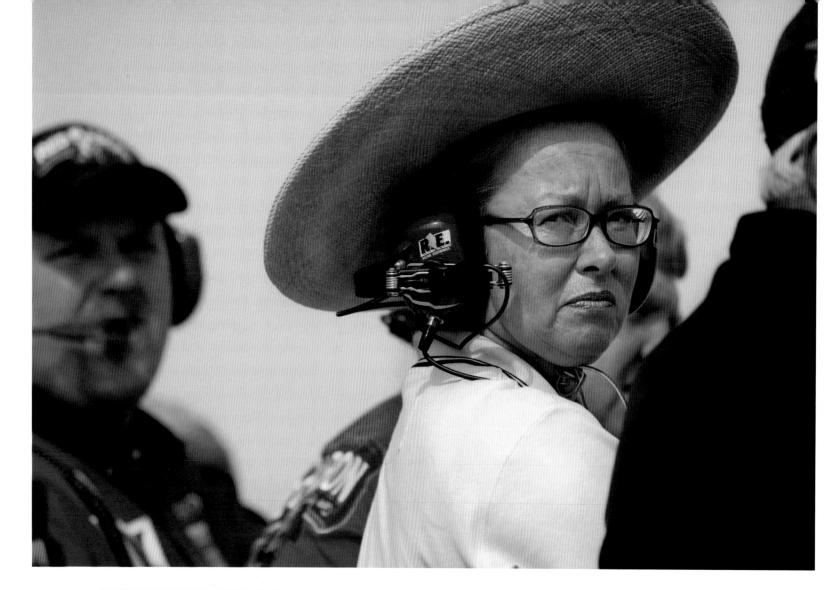

Beth Ann Morgenthau, owner of the BAM Racing team, atop the pit box for the No. 49 Red Baron car driven by Ken Schrader. Morgenthau, whose initials form the name of the operation, received the race team as a birthday present from her husband, Tony, in 2000.

Opposite page: Dale Earnhardt Jr. contemplates the upcoming MBNA RacePoints 400 at Dover, where he finished 31st in 2005.

Left: For each race, cars are fitted with a camera inside the trunk lid to give viewers at home a look at the action from every which angle.

Petty Enterprises crew chief Greg Steadman talks with longtime NASCAR commentator Berry Parsons as Steadman waits for the inspection of the No. 43 car, now driven by Bobby Labonte, to be completed at Talladega.

Opposite page: As part of pre-race inspection, officials check each car's body and parts to make sure they meet NASCAR standards. Using color-coded templates for each car make, officials can check the car's wing, bumper, and taillight to ensure no illegal modifications have been made.

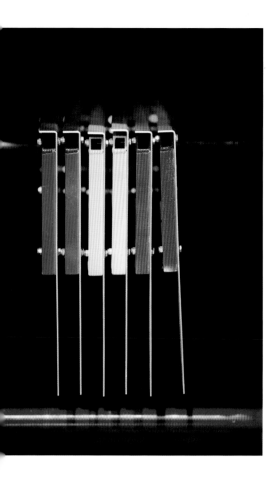

Small cans of sample gas are also taken from each car to check on race weekends as part of the inspection process.

Two track personnel overlook the action from the top of the stands at Dover.

A crew replaces lightbulbs on the position board at Talladega.

8   8

9   9

10   10

Sam Belnavis watches the action from Greg Biffle's pit area. He is the director of Roush's diversity program and is a co-sponsor of Biffle's car.

Michael Waltrip
Only as Good as Your Last Race

Minutes before NASCAR drivers fire up their engines and roar down pit lane, the scene is one of light-hearted banter. Some drivers horse around with their kids; others talk to the news media. Most have a smile and look utterly relaxed, as if they don't have a care in the world.

One of the earlier pictures in this book—of Michael Waltrip, one of the biggest names in NASCAR, kissing his wife Buffy just as a race was about to begin—made me think about pre-race rituals. I wondered what must go through a driver's mind in the moments before he climbs into his car and puts up the net.

When I met Waltrip in Daytona, I asked him about it. He rattled off a race morning to-do list as long as your arm, then offered up an image that seemed like a paradox: the race car as safe haven.

"It's just the nature of the business," Waltrip says, describing everything he does before the race begins. "We have to do interviews on the race morning. We have to do hospitality; we have to take care of our sponsors and meet with our teams. Then we go to the drivers' meetings and then we go to church. Then we go to a reception and then you get into the car, and it's your safe haven."

Sometimes, Waltrip says, his wife and two daughters write on his car or on his uniform, sending him little notes of encouragement. But after two decades of racing, he doesn't really need to psych himself up much on race day.

"It's automatic. You've got three laps behind the pace car to get to your road speed and get focused on what you're going to do," he says. "You already have thought about it all weekend. You don't need any pep talks. You've got it all in your brain. And then, when you get out of the car, you sort it all out."

That doesn't mean, though, that he never gets nervous behind the wheel.

"Who wouldn't? You're getting ready to race forty-two other guys down in a corner at two hundred miles an hour. That'll get your attention," he says. "But you have to control it. The first lap is not what pays. The last lap is. So you just chill out, race your butt off, and hopefully, you're around at the end."

Like all NASCAR drivers, Waltrip knows racing is dangerous work; he won one of his two Daytona 500 races the year Dale Earnhardt lost his life there. Still, he doesn't worry too much about himself.

"I've been doing this for twenty years, and you just race," he says. "And if you're going to wreck, you hang on, and hopefully you're okay. You go hug your wife and kids at the end."

But was there a single moment in that long racing career when Waltrip realized he had really arrived at NASCAR? The two-time Daytona 500 winner shakes his head at the question. "I always thought that any moment, I could be out of NASCAR," he says. "You're only as good as your last race."

Michael Waltrip hangs out with Morgan Shepherd before the Richmond race. Waltrip sees his time in the car as a safe haven from off-track demands on his time.

Robbie Reiser, crew chief for Matt Kenseth and the Roush Racing No. 17 car, at the Sony HD 500, where the team finished seventh in 2005.

Ron Malec, car chief for Jimmie Johnson and the No. 48 Lowe's Chevrolet, joined Hendrick Motorsports in 2001 as a team mechanic and rear tire carrier.

Opposite page: Kevin Buskirk, crew chief for Elliott Sadler, in the garage before the Richmond race in September 2005.

Dale Jarrett slides into the No. 88 UPS Ford before the September 2005 race at California, where his team finished 24th.

Opposite page: Bobby Labonte jokes around with fellow driver Matt Kenseth in September 2005 at Richmond, where both drivers had a good day. Kenseth finished second and Labonte came in ninth.

Johnny Benson climbs out of his car after a run at Lowe's Motor Speedway. In 10 years, Benson has competed in 271 NASCAR NEXTEL Cup races.

Opposite page: Jeff Burton, driver of the No. 31 Cingular Chevy, first started racing go karts when he was just seven years old. He won two state karting championships before moving to stock cars in 1984.

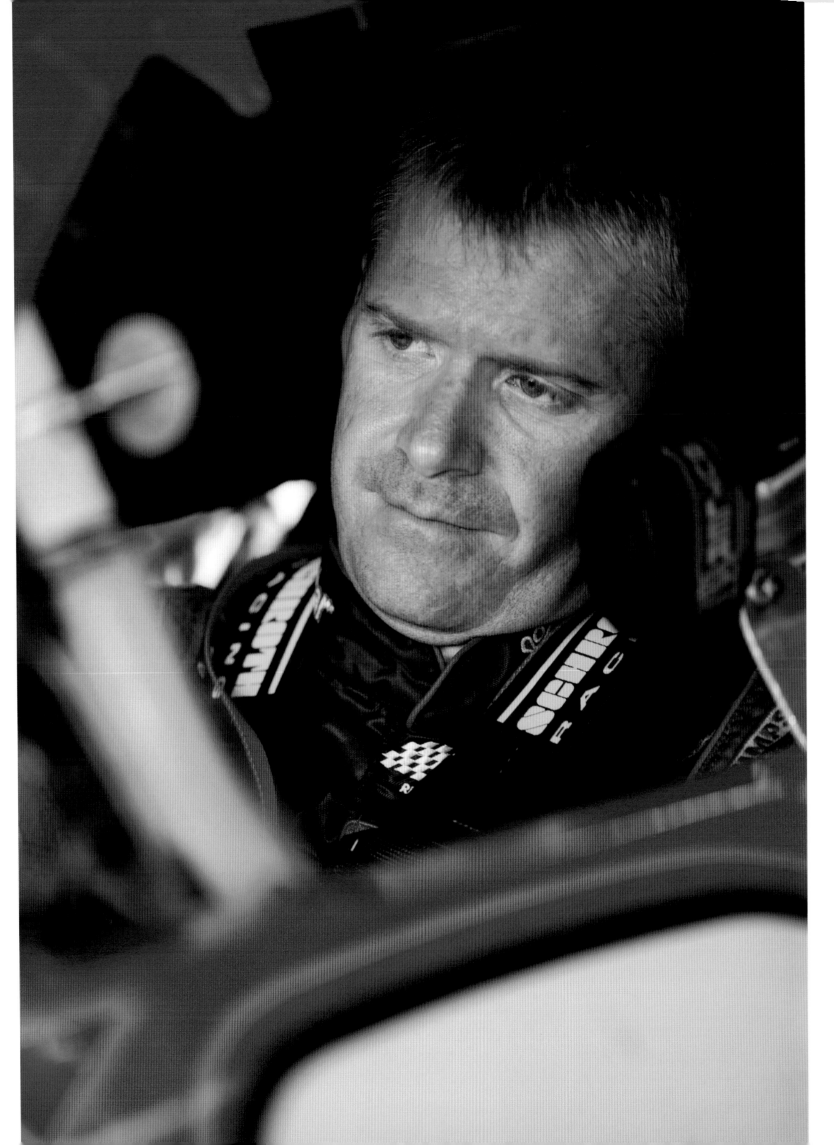

One NASCAR official keeps an eye on the racing action while another waves the green flag to open pit road during a race at Dover. At each event, about 40 officials oversee both the race preparations and the action on the track.

After driver Jeff Gordon was involved in a crash on Lap 65 in the 2005 UAW-Ford 500, the No. 24 DuPont crew went into action, quickly clearing out the pit box.

Thousands of fans watch the race in Dover, but the view from Ray Evernham's No. 9
pit box (there are only 43 of these at any NASCAR race) is every bit as exciting.

CHAPTER EIGHT
In the Spotlight

Claire B. Lang
A Broadcasting Trailblazer

Not long after I got my satellite radio, I was driving along, listening to the NASCAR channel, when I caught my first audio glimpse of Claire B. Lang. She seemed to be everywhere at the track: in the garage with a crew chief, on pit row with an owner, questioning a NASCAR official at one press conference or another. I turned to my photo assistant and said, "I've got to meet this Claire B. Lang."

So I did.

Claire calls herself "the hardest working person in NASCAR," and it's easy to see why. For four years, she's hosted the *Dialed In* show, beamed live coast to coast on XM Radio for three hours each afternoon. On weekends, she's off at the races, bringing fast-breaking news updates and pre- and post-race analysis to NASCAR fans around the country. She leaves her hotel at 6 a.m. and often doesn't return until 15 hours later.

In the mostly-male world of NASCAR, Claire is a trailblazer for women. Before XM existed, she was told that it would be many, many years before a woman would be on the radio networks covering NASCAR. Now she's a ubiquitous presence at the races, one of NASCAR's best-known unofficial personalities. Fans rely on her for the straight story. After all the other reporters are gone, Claire is the one hanging around the track, trying to nail down that last detail that brings her reporting to life.

Sometimes, she even makes the news herself, like the time Robby Gordon rebuffed press accounts that he pushed her while trying to avoid a mob of reporters. "I did not push Claire B. Lang after the race," Gordon declared, telling the press, "If she got moved a little bit, it was not an intentional shove. If I bumped you, I apologize."

Claire said at the time that she had no recollection of being pushed. It was a characteristically diplomatic comment, and she was equally diplomatic when I interviewed her in Daytona. She wouldn't dish on any of the drivers, wouldn't even tell me who her favorites were, though she did say she likes the young up-and-comers best.

"I have a special passion for the young drivers who come in that nobody knows," she says. "Everybody says, 'Who's your favorite driver?' I really tend to like the drivers that nobody can figure out. I like to try to unwrap them and portray their personalities so people can get to know them."

For Claire, good radio is like fine art; the best reporters are "painting that perfect picture in sound." One word she uses a lot is *trust*. "I want listeners to trust me," she says, "that what they're hearing is not something to make the phones ring, but as close as I can get to all aspects of the truth."

Another word she likes is *respect*. "What I care most about is that I have the respect of the listeners and the competitors, and that I leave a good legacy for the young girls who come after me. That's huge to me."

Claire B. Lang, XM Radio's NASCAR reporter, spends much of her time at the track with her trusty notebook and digital recorder, getting interviews for her race reports and information for her *Dialed In* program.

Richard Petty addressing the media with other team owners at a Daytona Speedweeks press conference. He won his first race as an owner in 1996, with driver Bobby Hamilton behind the wheel.

After an early NASCAR Busch Series wreck at Dover in 2005, Matt Kenseth and Michael Waltrip watch the replay for the first time while giving a trackside interview. Four other drivers also had to end their racing day on Lap 1.

As NASCAR has continued to draw a larger and larger fan base, more media attention has been focused on the sport. At each race, an entourage of reporters, photographers, and camera operators are on hand to record the action.

Opposite page: Popular drivers like Tony Stewart often have more time to sign autographs for fans before NASCAR Busch Series races. In 2005 and 2006, he captured two NASCAR Busch Series wins.

Jeff Gordon signs a No. 24 visor for a fan while standing backstage before driver introductions. He finished seccond in the fan voting for the most popular driver award in 2005.

Opposite page: Driver Dave Blaney signs for fans at Talladega. He recorded six top-10 finishes in his second season in NASCAR NEXTEL Cup, a career high.

Scott Wimmer
Scribbling Signatures

Scott Wimmer learned the importance of fans back when he was just a teenager, trying to carve out a racing career on small-town tracks in his home state of Wisconsin. This was in the early 1990s, long before Wimmer caught the eye of top NASCAR owners and just before America's interest in stock car racing really exploded.

"It was a whole different set of fans," Wimmer remembers. "We had a group of fans that would follow the drivers to the different tracks. You really got to know them on a personal level. You could sit down after a race and talk with fans for two hours. It was a lot of personal time with the fans, which is the biggest difference I see [compared to NASCAR racing]."

Indeed, even lesser-known NASCAR drivers like Wimmer, who finished 32nd in 2005, are mobbed by fans from the moment they arrive at a race until the moment they leave. Wimmer says every race is a tug of emotions. He always wants to stay until the last autograph has been signed, but time is always short. There is always a public relations person trailing him, pulling him away, telling him it's time to go. Sometimes it can feel a little overwhelming.

"Now we're going to venues where we'll have over one hundred thousand people," he says. "It just takes some time to get used to. It's a little weird going down pit row at Talladega and seeing ten thousand or fifteen thousand fans. You try to get to everybody, but ultimately you just can't do it."

This image of Wimmer came from that very spot, pit row at Talladega, where he finished 17th, one of his best showings for 2005. It was before the October race, and he didn't seem to be anxious or in a rush. He just moved methodically from one eager autograph-seeker to the next, happy to oblige their requests for him to sign hats, T-shirts, pennants, even body parts.

In this shot, Wimmer is signing a woman's visor, offering a hint at an important NASCAR trend: the ever-increasing numbers of female fans, who are changing the demographics of the sport and broadening its reach. NASCAR estimates that women now make up 40 percent of its fan base.

"I've signed anywhere—from people's arms, their shirts, their hats, to dollar bills, five-dollar bills," Wimmer says. "To me, that was probably the strangest request I've ever had."

Since he signed on with NASCAR in late 2003, Wimmer has written his name for eager fans so many times, and in so many different places, that his signature is not what it was back in the days when he was tooling around the small-town tracks of Wisconsin.

"My autograph's gotten terrible over the years," he confesses. "It seems like we'll do anything to get it quicker and faster. I used to do all the *M*s on *Wimmer*, and now it's just a straight line."

Scott Wimmer moves down the line, signing autographs for many fans, including one admirer who asked him to sign her visor at Talladega. He says he uses up a lot more ink now than he did during his early driving days in Wisconsin.

Saturday Night Live alum Will Ferrell gets serious as he plays the role of rebel driver Ricky Bobby in *Talladega Nights: The Ballad of Ricky Bobby*. In the NASCAR-themed film, Ricky Bobby wins the hearts of fans with his "win at all costs" approach to racing.

Fellow *Talladega Nights* cast member John C. Reilly plays the role of Cal Naughton Jr., Ricky Bobby's loyal racing partner and childhood friend. Their motto while driving on the track is "Shake and Bake."

Kyle Petty hangs out on the top of a Petty Enterprises hauler behind the watchful eye of the camera at Richmond, where he finished 27th in the 2005 Chevy Rock & Roll 400.

Night falls on California Speedway, putting the track in the spotlight for the rest of the race.

Mike Helton, president of NASCAR, often discusses rule changes, safety policies, and the racing schedule and format to members of the media, drivers, and team owners. At the end of 2004, he helped launch the Chase for the NASCAR NEXTEL Cup, restarting the points race in the last 10 races of the schedule.

Opposite page: Owner Richard Childress speaks to the media at Lowe's Motor Speedway's press building.

CHAPTER NINE

Changing of the Guard

Kim Crosby gave up her full-time job as a junior high school principal to become a full-time NASCAR driver in 2004. Before competing in stock car races, Crosby made a name for herself in drag racing.

Opposite page: Erin Crocker is all smiles before driver introductions at a NASCAR Busch Series race at Dover. She is the newest woman to get behind the wheel to compete and owner Ray Evernham now backs her in a full NASCAR Busch schedule.

Jamie McMurray, one of the younger NASCAR NEXTEL Cup drivers, switched teams at the end of 2005, joining powerhouse Roush Racing in the hopes of furthering his career.

Casey Mears, nephew of four-time Indy 500 winner Rick Mears, has been racing in the NASCAR NEXTEL Cup Series for four years and is still waiting to claim his first win.

While Tony Stewart has already won two NASCAR NEXTEL Cup championships, he's still one of the younger drivers who competes to win each week.

Even on a cloudy day at Pocono, Kyle Busch has his sunglasses on. In just his second year competing at NASCAR's highest level, he won two races.

Opposite page: Ryan Newman has become known for his ability to win the pole in his first five full-time years racing in NASCAR NEXTEL Cup. He has a degree in vehicle structure engineering, which probably helps him get his car setup just right before qualifying.

Kyle's brother Kurt won a NASCAR NEXTEL Cup Series championship at the age of 26, after only four years racing in the series.

Denny Hamlin is one of the NASCAR NEXTEL Cup rookies in 2006. He outpaced many veterans to a 10th-place finish at the UAW-DaimlerChrysler 400, the season's third race.

Driver Kevin Harvick racked up four wins in just three years when he first entered the NASCAR NEXTEL Cup scene.

Epilogue
A New Vision of the Sport

When I came up with the idea for Faces of NASCAR, I wanted to focus solely on portraits. Portraits of drivers, of crew chiefs, of tire specialists, of fans—portraits the faces that I knew lurked behind the walls of the NASCAR nation.

But when I arrived at Pocono in July of 2005 for my very first *Faces of NASCAR* shoot, a different face of NASCAR caught my eye.

One of the first things I noticed, and was shocked by, was the sheer physical beauty of the venue. It was filled with color and graphic angles, striking elements that combined to tell the NASCAR story in a very different way than I had anticipated. During some downtime between shooting portraits of Kyle Busch and Brian Vickers, I began to explore the landscape.

I captured, from afar, the sight of an older couple sitting atop the grandstands—on a simple piece of plywood painted St. Patrick's Day emerald green. I trained my lens close up on a sea of tires, set against a stark Pocono sign. I shot a geometric image of a series of haulers—a simple photograph of one truck lined up next to another next to another, with a huge American flag looming overhead, its red and blue stripes set off against a clear blue sky.

The pictures didn't seem to fit with my *Faces of NASCAR* theme, but I found myself drawn to these graphic elements at every track I visited. Eventually, I came up with a name for this series: ScottVision, a play on SpeedVision, a cable channel now known as Speed TV that most NASCAR fans are intimately familiar with.

At California Motor Speedway, I shot a night scene as I stood beside my rental car, before packing up to leave the track. The good light for shooting portraits was long gone, but as I gathered my bags, I looked over my shoulder and saw the darkening sky contrasted against the lights of the track.

In Daytona, I left the track through the Turn Four tunnel and was struck by its checkerboard interior. I had arrived earlier that day through other side of that same tunnel; the entrance was painted green. How clever, I thought, to fashion the tunnel décor after the flags used to start and finish the race.

At Talladega, while walking in the infield one night, I stumbled upon a catering truck advertising what seemed an odd combination: tobacco and snacks. Patrons were swarming the tobacco snack wagon like moths around a light. I set up a tripod and captured the scene on a time exposure.

ScottVision was one of the biggest surprises of *Faces of NASCAR*, and in the end, it allowed me to expand my thinking about what the title of this book was really about. In the broadest sense, NASCAR's face is not only a human one. The racetracks themselves, each with its own personality and characteristics, are also, in a very real way, the faces of NASCAR.

A row of haulers in the infield. On average, the drivers of these transporters log 70,000 miles behind the wheel each season.

Opposite page: A sea of tires at Pocono.

A glowing tobacco and snack stand at Talladega.

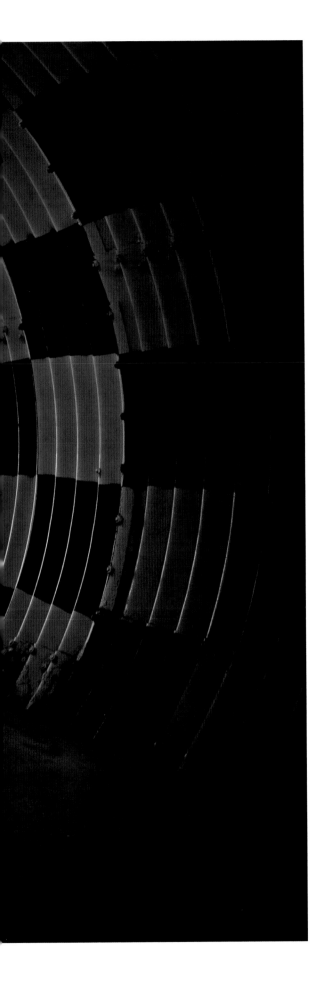

The Daytona International Speedway, the premier track in NASCAR, has a checkered flag tunnel leading out of its infield at Turn Four.

Massive custom semis (above) shine brightly in the California sun.

Four seats lined up to give fans the ultimate "Garage – Vu."

Acknowledgments

I began this project knowing a lot about photography, but little about book publishing or NASCAR. A number of people helped me along the way, and I would like to thank them here, beginning with Randy Leffingwell. Without Randy, this book would not have been possible. His able guidance led me to the wonderful team of editors at MBI Publishing Company, including the ever-patient Leah Noel.

I am also grateful to the folks at NASCAR, who took a chance on a book that featured people, not cars, and thankful for all the drivers, crew chiefs, public relations people, and fans who made the work so much fun. Two especially stand out: Diane Hawkins and Chris Haid, who fielded numerous phone calls and never failed to answer my NASCAR questions.

My longtime friends Alan Dorrow, Gordon Joffrion, and Walt Stricklin, all wonderful photographers in their own right, offered creative and technical assistance, sprinkled with good humor. My neighbor, the gifted writer Lucy Harvey, was a coach extraordinaire. My parents, David and Audrey Robinson, provided a steady stream of hometown news clippings to keep me up to date on Kentuckians in NASCAR.

But most of all, I'd like to thank my loving family—my beautiful daughters Olivia and Hannah Robinson, who didn't complain (much) about Dad missing their fall soccer season while off at the races, and my wife, Sheryl Gay Stolberg, whose unending support and calming influence is always a source of comfort.

—Scott Robinson

Index